Know About Great Inventors Of The World

MAPLE KIDS

Published by

MAPLE PRESS PRIVATE LIMITED
office: A-63, Sector 58, Noida 201301, U.P., India
phone: +91 120 455 3581, 455 3583
email: info@maplepress.co.in
website: www.maplepress.co.in
Go to www.maplelibrary.com for more e-books.

Reprinted in 2019

ISBN: 978-93-50335-69-7

Contents

Preface 4

1. Archimedes 5

2. Charles Babbage 8

3. John Logie Baird 12

4. Graham Bell 15

5. Herbert Boyer and Stanley Cohen 19

6. Marie Curie 22

7. Leonardo da Vinci 25

8. Walt Disney 29

9. George Eastman 32

10. Thomas Edison 35

11. Albert Einstein 38

12. Michael Faraday 41

13. Alexander Fleming 44

14. Henry Ford 47

15. Galileo Galilei 50

16. Guglielmo Marconi 54

17. James Clerk Maxwell 57

18. Sir Isaac Newton 59

19. Alfred Nobel 63

20. Louis Pasteur 66

21. Blaise Pascal 69

22. Percy L. Spencer 72

23. Wright Brothers 75

24. James Watt 79

Preface

Have you ever imagined your life without electric lights, washing machines, cars or computers? Every invention and discovery highly influences our world and our lives.

In this book, we will venture through the lives of some great inventors to witness how they achieved their goals. Take a moment to think about which inventions are most important to you. On this adventurous trip of exploration, you might discover how these inventions were created! It's all about clarity, precision and curiosity that have led these inventors to come up with some greatest scientific discoveries and inventions.

The book sums up some of the famous inventors of the world. It includes their background, their achievements and their contributions to mankind. Hope you have a great read!

Chapter 1

Archimedes

Archimedes is considered as one of the greatest mathematicians in history and is counted among the three greatest mathematicians, Isaac Newton and Carl Gauss. In the field of mathematics, he is known for his contributions in the field of geometry. From his early years, Archimedes was passionately obsessed with Geometry.

Archimedes was born in Syracuse, Greece in 287 BC. He died in 212 BC while he was in the middle of solving a mathematical problem. He was killed by a Roman soldier who did not recognize Archimedes and pierced

his sword through him after Archimedes denied meeting General Marcellus.

Archimedes was the son of an astronomer named Phidias. He received his formal education in Alexandria, Egypt, which was considered as the 'intellectual centre' of the world. After completing his formal studies in

Alexandria, he returned and stayed in Syracuse for the rest of his life. There is no recorded information about his personal life or marriage.

Contributions

• Archimedes discovered how to find the *volume of a sphere* and determined the exact *value of Pi*.

• Famously known as the *Archimedes' principle*, he discovered the 'Principle of Buoyancy'. It is believed that he was so happy to discover this principle that without realizing, he ran through the streets naked shouting '*Eureka*' which meant 'I have found it'.

• It is believed that Archimedes was the first to have invented '*Integral Calculus*' even before Newton and Leibniz.

• He invented a way to calculate the '*powers of ten*'. It refers to the number of zeroes in a number. He thus contributed to the advancement in the Greek numerical system which eliminated the use of the Greek alphabet in the counting system.

• He also invented the formula to find the exact amount of *area enclosed by a curve*.

Famous quotes:

• "Eureka"- I have found it!

• "Don't disturb my circles!"

• "Give me a place to stand, and I will move the earth."

Chapter 2
Charles Babbage

Charles Babbage was born in London on 26 December 1791. During his early years he suffered from a fatal fever and was sent to a clergy operated school for special care.

Babbage was lucky to have a wealthy father who encouraged him for further studies. Therefore, he joined Holmwood Academy in Baker Street, Middlesex. Here, he gradually developed an interest in Mathematics. He was provided schooling and tutoring at home so that he would get accepted in Cambridge.

Babbage enjoyed reading many of the major works in mathematics and showed remarkable understanding of the theories and ideas. He was influenced by a French mathematician, Lacroix. He focused on his works on differential and integral calculus. Later, Babbage was asked to set up an Analytical Society solely consisting of Cambridge undergraduates. The group consisted of Babbage, John Herschel and George Peacock and focused

on serious publications in this period. Many leading math scholars praised Babbage for his contributions.

Charles completed his schooling and started to write papers on various subjects for the Royal Society of London. They honored him with an invitation to join as the Vice-President. Babbage became interested in the study of astronomy and in the equipments used to study the outer space. Frustrated with the waste of time and money used to create a logarithmic table manually, Babbage invented the *Difference Machine* to create these tables. The success of this endeavor led Babbage to envision a device that could perform any possible calculation.

For the making of the *Analytical Engine*, Babbage received funding from the government to turn his dream into reality. Unfortunately, Babbage was never able to finish the project, as the project was dismissed after a few flawed programs were tested. The process and structure of the engine formed the foundation of the calculation process in modern computers.

His Contributions:

- Table of Logarithms of the Natural Numbers from 1 to 108, 000
  - Reflections on the Decline of Science in England
  - On the Economy of Machinery and Manufactures
  - Ninth Bridgewater Treatise
  - Passages from the Life of a Philosopher

Famous quotes:

- "As soon as an Analytical Engine exists, it will necessarily guide the future course of science."
- What is there in a name? It is merely an empty basket, until you put something into it."
- If we look at the fact, we shall find that the great inventions of the age are not, with us at least, always produced in universities.

Chapter 3

John Logie Baird

John Logie Baird was born on 13 August 1888 in Helensburgh, Scotland and died on 14 June 1946 in Sussex, England. John Logie Baird received a diploma degree in Electrical Engineering at the Glasgow and West of Scotland Technical College and pursued his Bachelors of Science in Electrical Engineering from the University

of Glasgow, and had to leave his studies midway due to the outbreak of World War I.

John Logie Baird is best remembered as the inventor of mechanical television system. In 1920's, John Logie Baird and American Clarence W. Hansell patented the idea of using arrays of transparent rods to transmit images for television and copy machines, respectively.

In 1924, he created the first televised pictures of objects in motion, the first televised human face in 1925 and the first moving object image at the Royal Institution in London in 1926. In 1928, his trans-atlantic transmission of the image of a human face was a broadcasting milestone.

Color television, stereoscopic television and television by infrared light were all demonstrated by Baird before 1930. He successfully lobbied for broadcast time with

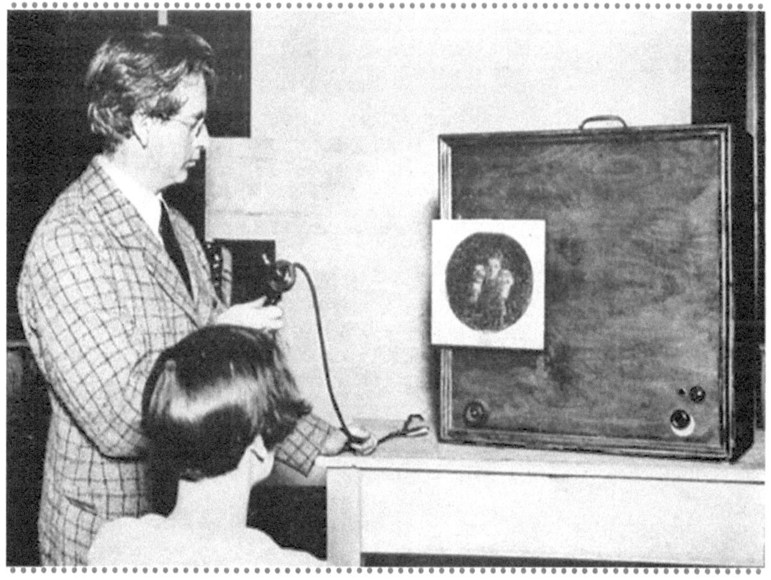

the British Broadcasting Company and the BBC started broadcasting television on Baird's 30 line system in 1929. The first simultaneous sound and vision telecast was broadcasted in 1930.

In 1936, the British Broadcasting Corporation adopted television service using the electronic television technology of Marconi-EMI. It was the world's first regular high resolution service with 405 lines per picture which won over Baird's system.

Famous quote:

• Cathode-ray tubes are the most important items in a television receiver.

Chapter 4

Graham Bell

In the 1870s, two inventors, Elisha Gray and Alexander Graham Bell, independently designed the 'telephone' that could transmit speech electrically. Both rushed their respective designs to the patent office within hours of each other. Alexander Graham Bell patented his telephone first. This resulted in the famous legal battle between Elisha Gray and Alexander Graham Bell over the invention of the telephone. At last, Bell won.

The telegraph and telephone are both wire-based electrical systems. Alexander Graham Bell's success with the telephone resulted from his efforts to improve the telegraph.

When Bell began experimenting with electrical signals, the telegraph had already been an established means of communication for about 30 years. Though it was highly successful, the telegraph was limited to receiving and sending one message at a time. Bell's extensive knowledge of the nature of sounds and his understanding of music enabled him to guess the possibility of sending multiple

messages, over the same wire, at the same time. Although the idea of a multiple telegraph had been in existence for some time, Bell offered his own musical approach as a possible practical solution. His 'harmonic telegraph' worked on the principle of transmitting several notes simultaneously along the same wire, if the notes or signals differed in pitch.

By October 1874, Bell's research had progressed to such an extent that he could inform his future father-in-law, Gardiner Greene Hubbard, about the possibility of a multiple telegraph. Hubbard, who resented the absolute control that was exerted by the Western Union Telegraph Company gave Bell the necessary financial backing he needed. Bell along with Thomas Watson, a young electrician, proceeded with his work on 'multiple telegraph'. But he did not tell Hubbard that he and Thomas Watson were simply exploring an idea that had occurred to him that summer - of developing a device that would transmit speech electrically.

On 2 June 1875, while experimenting with his technique of 'harmonic telegraph', Alexander Graham Bell discovered that he could hear sounds over the wire. The sound was that of a twanging clock spring.

10 March 1876 marked the birth of the telephone but death of the 'multiple telegraph'. This was accounted as

one of his greatest successes. The effective communicative technique of being able to 'talk with electricity' cancelled out all implications of the dot-and-dash system.

The notebook entry of Alexander Graham Bell's on the same date, describes his successful experiment with the telephone. Speaking to his assistant through the instrument, Bell uttered these famous first words, *"Mr. Watson — come here — I want to see you."*

Alexander Graham Bell was born on 3 March 1847 in Edinburgh, Scotland. He belonged to a family of elocutionists who dealt in phonetics and correction of speech. Educated to pursue his career in the same specialty, his knowledge of the nature of sounds led him not only to teach the deaf, but also to invent the telephone.

Bell's unceasing scientific curiosity led to the invention of 'photophone'. He also developed his own flying machine, just six years after the Wright Brothers launched their plane at Kitty Hawk. As President James Garfield lay dying of an assassin's bullet in 1881, Bell hurriedly invented a metal detector in an unsuccessful attempt to locate the fatal bullet.

Famous quotes:

• When one door closes another door opens; but we so often look so long and so regretfully upon the closed door, that we do not see the ones which open for us.

• Before anything else, preparation is the key to success.

Chapter 5

Herbert Boyer and Stanley Cohen

In 1973, Herbert Boyer and Stanley Cohen invented the technique of DNA cloning, which allowed genes to be transplanted between different biological species. Their discovery indicated the birth of genetic engineering.

Herbert Boyer and Stanley Cohen combined their efforts to invent a method of cloning where genetically arranged molecules are inserted into foreign cells. With

this discovery and its applications, Boyer and Cohen developed what is now a multibillion-dollar biotechnology industry.

Their collaboration began at a conference in Hawaii in 1972. Boyer was a biochemist and genetic engineer at the University of California at San Francisco and Cohen was an associate professor of medicine at Stanford University. Within four months, the joint effort of Boyer's and Cohen's labs succeeded in cloning predetermined patterns of DNA. Their joint work resulted in the making of dozens of medical products including synthetic insulin for diabetes, a clot-dissolving agent for heart-attack victims and a growth hormone for underdeveloped children. In addition to these, a number of lifesaving substances are now produced worldwide by Boyer's and Cohen's cloning methodology.

Herbert Boyce and Stanley Cohen were awarded the 1996 Lemelson-MIT Prize for Invention and Innovation for their spirited teamwork, entrepreneurship and vehement dedication which helped them to achieve success.

Famous quotes:

- The great aim of education is not knowledge but action.

- Education has for its object the formation of character.

Chapter 6
Marie Curie

Dr. Marie Curie is known to the world as a famous scientist who discovered radioactive metals like Radium and Polonium.

Marie Curie was a Polish physicist and chemist who lived from 7 November 1867 to 4 July 1934. Together with her husband, Pierre, she discovered radium and polonium. By the end of World War I, Marie Curie was probably the most famous woman in the world.

As a child, Marie Curie amazed people with the sharpness of her memory. She learned to read when she was only four years old. Her father was a Professor of Science and the instruments that he kept in a glass case fascinated Marie. She dreamt of becoming a scientist, but that would not be easy. Her family became very poor and at the age of 18, Marie became a governess. She helped to pay for her sister to study in Paris. Later, her sister helped Marie with her education. In 1891, Marie attended the Sorbonne University in Paris, where she met and married Pierre Curie, a well-known physicist.

Her co-discovery of radium and polonium with her husband Pierre Curie represents one of the best known stories in modern science. Recognizing their contribution in the field of science, they were awarded with the Nobel Prize in Physics in 1901. In 1911, Marie Curie was honoured with a second Nobel Prize in Chemistry.

After the sudden accidental death of Pierre Curie, Marie Curie single-handedly raised her two daughters,

Irene and Eve (Irene, who also won a Nobel Prize in Chemistry in 1935 and Eve who became an accomplished author) and continued building an active career in experimental radioactive measurements.

She died of leukemia caused by repeated exposure to radioactive materials.

Famous quotes:

• Nothing in life is to be feared, it is only to be understood. Now is the time to understand more, so that we may fear less.

• Be less curious about people and more curious about ideas.

• I was taught that the way of progress was neither swift nor easy.

Chapter 7
Leonardo da Vinci

Leonardo da Vinci was a versatile genius who had studied and contributed in almost every field of knowledge including anatomy, physiology, mechanics, hydraulics, physics, philosophy, mathematics, writing and engineering, orbital mechanics, botany, optics. Apart from being regarded as the greatest painters of all times, he has earned the epithet as the 'Universal Genius'.

Leonardo da Vinci formally studied about flights in 1480's. He had over 100 drawings that illustrated his theories on flight.

The Ornithopter flying machine was never actually created. It was a design that Leonardo da Vinci created to show how man could fly. The modern day helicopter is based on this concept.

Artists have always found it difficult to make a living off their art. Even a master like Leonardo was forced to sell out, in order to support himself, so he adapted his drawing skills to more profitable fields of architecture, military engineering, canal building and weapons design.

He worked for the Duke of Milan and called himself a military engineer and outlined some of his ideas for weapons. He briefly mentioned to the Duke that he could paint as well.

Luckily for Leonardo, he was actually talented as an engineer. Though good illustrators were available in Renaissance Italy, but Leonardo had the brains and the diligence to break new grounds, and his brilliance shone brightly against everyone else.

Nearly a century before Galileo, Leonardo butted heads with the challenge of measuring time. For him, the most interesting part was the use of mechanical gears and he studied them with relish. During his lifetime, he invented the bicycle, a helicopter, an 'auto mobile' and some gruesome weapons.

Leonardo also studied all forms of water, i.e., liquid, steam and ice. His curious mind had all sort of ideas of what to do with it. He invented a device to measure humidity, steam-powered cannon, many different waterwheels and several forms of useful industrial machines which extracted its power from flowing water. He forever imagined things like floating snowshoes to walk on water, breathing devices and webbed gloves to explore underwater, a life preserver to remain afloat, devices to attack and sink ships from underwater and an 'unsinkable' double-hulled ship.

Leonardo da Vinci was born on 15 April 1452 in Florence and died on 2 May 1519 due to recurrent

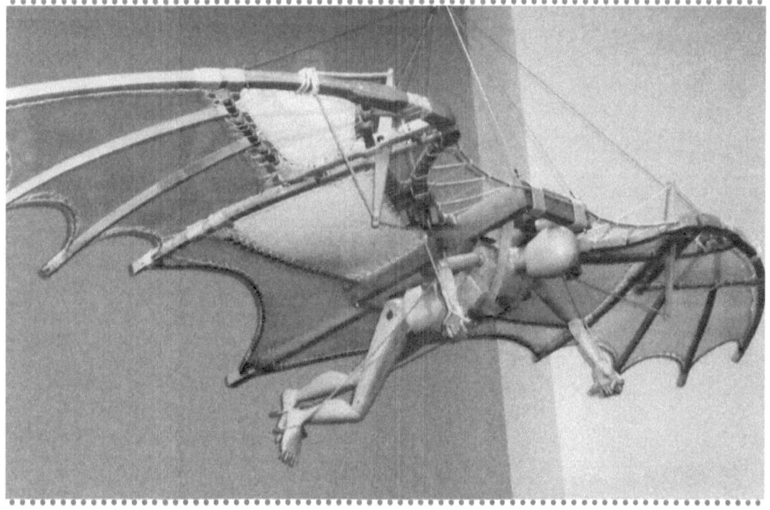

strokes. Nevertheless, he marked a distinct reign with his inquisitiveness, vehemence, theories and contributions.

Famous quotes:

- Simplicity is the ultimate sophistication.
- Art is never finished, only abandoned.

Chapter 8
Walt Disney

Walt Disney, the creator of Mickey Mouse, founder of the Disneyland and Walt Disney World Theme Parks, was born in Chicago on 5 December 1901. His father, Elias Disney, was Irish-Canadian whereas his mother, Flora Call Disney, was of German-American descent.

During a 43-year Hollywood career that spanned to the development of the motion picture medium as a modern American art, Walter Elias Disney, established himself and his product as a genuine part of America. David Low, the late British political cartoonist, called Disney "the most significant figure in graphic arts since Leonardo"

A pioneer and innovator of one of the most fertile imaginations that the world has ever known, Walt Disney, along with the members of his staff, received more than 950 honours and citations from every nation in the world. He won 48 Academy Awards and seven Emmys in his lifetime. Walt Disney's personal awards included honorary degrees from Harvard, Yale, the University

of Southern California and UCLA, the Presidential Medal of Freedom, France's Legion of Honour and Officer d'Academic decorations, Thailand's Order of the Crown, Brazil's Order of the Southern Cross, Mexico's Order of the Aztec Eagle and the Showman of the World Award from the National Association of Theatre Owners.

Walt Disney invented the multiplane camera. The multiplane camera was used in the Walt Disney Studios during the thirties and forties to create countless animated pictures. The multi-plane used stacked planes of glass, each painted with different elements of the animation.

According to Disney World, "Mickey Mouse's official birthday is on 18 November 1928, when he made his first film debut in Steamboat Willie. This was the first Mickey Mouse cartoon released." Mickey Mouse's image is the most reproduced in the world. Over 7,500 items bear his likeness. Jesus is number two and Elvis is number three.

Famous quotes:

• All our dreams can come true, if we have the courage to pursue them.

• It's kind of fun to do the impossible.

• I only hope that we never lose sight of one thing- that it was all started by a mouse.

Chapter 9

George Eastman

A passionate photographer and the founder of Eastman Kodak Company, George Eastman, invented rolled photographic film. In 1888, he also invented the Kodak cameras that could use the new film. "*You press the button, we do the rest*" promised George Eastman while advertising for his Kodak camera.

Eastman wanted to simplify the photographic process and make it available to common man. 'Kodak' was founded in 1888. Pre-loaded with enough film for 100 exposures, the camera was portable and could be easily operated. After exposure, the camera was returned to the company in Rochester, New York, where the film was developed, prints were made; new films were inserted and returned back to the customer. Through a combination of research, experimentation and entrepreneurship, George Eastman, revolutionized photography and founded one of the world's best-known corporations.

In 1877, Eastman began his work in photography. However, inspired by an article in a British almanac,

Eastman dreamt of creating a 'dry plate' developing process. Dry film would make the developing process comparatively simpler and could be used in smaller and lighter cameras. Within a span of two years, Eastman built a 'Method and Apparatus for Coating Plates' which made dry film a reality.

Further innovations followed. In 1885, Eastman began marketing the world's first commercial film which was transparent and flexible in form.

In his own words, *"The letter 'K' had been a favorite with me—it seems a strong, incisive sort of letter. It became a question of trying out a great number of combinations of letters that made words starting and ending with 'K'"*

Eastman was one of the first American industrialists to employ a full-time research scientist. Together with his associate, Eastman perfected the first commercial transparent roll film, which led to the invention of Thomas Edison's motion picture camera in 1891.

On 26 April 1976, one of the largest patent suits involving photography was filed in the U.S. District Court of Massachusetts. Polaroid Corporation brought an action against Kodak Corporation for violation of 12 Polaroid patents. On 11 October 1985, after five years of vigorous pre-trial activity and 75 days of trial, seven Polaroid patents were found to be infringed. Kodak was out of the instant picture market, leaving customers with useless cameras and no film. Kodak variedly compensated camera owners for their loss.

Famous quotes:

• You press the button, we do the rest.

• What we do during our working hours determines what we have; what we do in our leisure hours determines what we are.

Chapter 10
Thomas Edison

Popularly known as America's greatest inventor, Thomas Alva Edison's first great invention was the tin foil phonograph which he developed in Menlo Park. While working to improve the efficiency of a telegraph transmitter, he noted that the tape of the machine gave off a noise similar to spoken words, when played at a high speed. This made him wonder about the possibility to record a telephone message.

He began experimenting with the diaphragm of a telephone receiver by attaching a needle to it. His experiments led him to try a stylus on a tinfoil cylinder, which, to his great surprise, played back the short message he had recorded, 'Mary had a little lamb'.

The word 'phonograph' was used as the trade name for Edison's device, which played cylinders rather than discs. This was the first machine that could record and reproduce sound. The machine had two needles, one for recording and one for playback. When you spoke into the

mouthpiece, the sound vibrations of your voice would be transferred onto the cylinder by the recording needle. This cylinder created a sensation and brought Edison international fame.

According to the recorded facts, Thomas Edison successfully completed the model of his first phonograph on 12 August 1877. He toured around the country with the tin foil phonograph and was invited to the White House to demonstrate it to President Rutherford B. Haves in April 1878.

In 1878, Thomas Edison established the Edison Speaking Phonograph Company. He suggested other uses for the phonograph, such as letter writing and dictation, phonographic books for blind people, a family record which recorded their voices, music boxes and toys, clocks that announced time and a telephone connection so that communications could be recorded.

Famous quotes:

- I have not failed. I've found 10,000 ways that won't work.

- Genius is one percent inspiration and ninety-nine percent perspiration.

Chapter 11
Albert Einstein

Albert Einstein was born in Germany on 14 March 1879. He enjoyed classical music and played the violin. During his early years, he was fascinated by the magnetic compass. The needle's invariable northward swing, guided by an invisible force, profoundly impressed the child. The compass convinced him that there had to be *'something behind things, something deeply hidden'*.

Even as a small boy, Albert Einstein was self-sufficient and thoughtful. He was a slow talker, pausing to consider what he would say. His sister remembered the concentration with which he used to build the house of cards.

Albert Einstein's first job was that of patent clerk.

In 1933, he joined the staff of the newly created Institute for Advanced Study in Princeton, New Jersey. He accepted this position for life, living there until his death. Einstein is probably familiar to most people for his mathematical equation about the nature of energy, $E = MC2$ which is regarded as *"world's most famous equation"*.

Einstein was asked to become the President of Israel which he politely declined. He was awarded the Nobel Prize in 1921 for his contributions in Theoretical Physics. After his death in 1955, his brain was stolen during autopsy at Princeton Hospital by Thomas Harvey, the postmortem surgeon, who was later fired from his job.

Albert Einstein is often regarded as the Father of Modern Science.

Famous quotes:

- Imagination is more important than knowledge.

- Life is like riding a bicycle. To keep your balance you must keep moving.

Chapter 12
Michael Faraday

Michael Faraday was a British physicist and chemist, best known for his discoveries of *electromagnetic induction* and of the laws of electrolysis. His biggest breakthrough in electricity was his invention of the electric motor.

Known to be extremely curious and inquisitive, Michael Faraday was born on 22 September 1791 in London. He always felt an urgent need to know more. At a tender age of 13, he became an errand boy for a bookbinding shop in London. He read every book that he found and decided that one day he would write a book of his own. He became interested in the concept of energy, specifically force.

Due to his early readings, interests and experiments with the idea of force, he was able to make important discoveries in electricity later in his life. He eventually became a well-known chemist and physicist and contributed to the understanding of electromagnetism.

Michael Faraday built two devices to produce 'electromagnetic rotation'. Ten years later, in 1831, he

began his great series of experiments which led him to discover 'electromagnetic induction'. These experiments formed the basis of modern electromagnetic technology.

Michael Faraday continued with his electrical experiments. In 1832, he proved that the electricity produced from a magnet, voltaic electricity produced by a battery and static electricity was all the same. He also significantly contributed in electrochemistry, stating the First and Second Laws of Electrolysis.

Famous quotes:

• There's nothing quite as frightening as someone who knows they are right.

• Nothing is too wonderful to be true if it be consistent with the laws of nature.

• But still try for who knows what is possible!

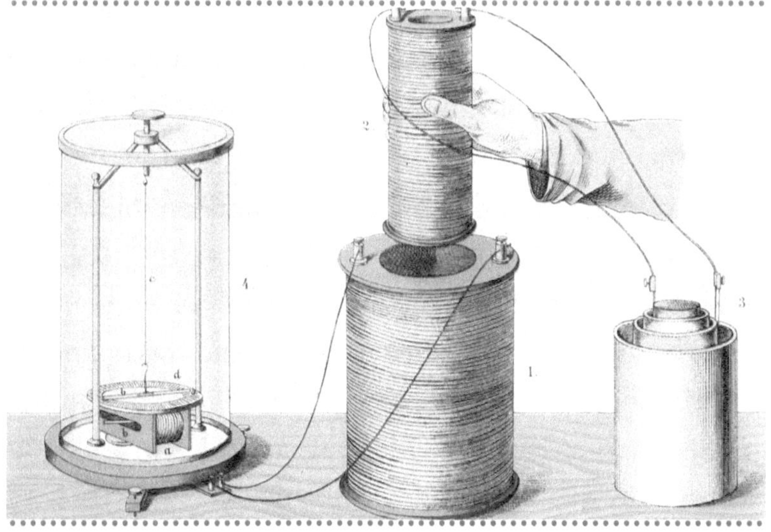

Chapter 13
Alexander Fleming

Famously known as the 'discoverer of penicillin', Alexander Fleming was born on 6 August 1881 in Ayrshire, Scotland. The Fleming children spent much of their time ranging through the streams, valleys and moors of the countryside. Recollecting his childhood days, Fleming said "we unconsciously learned a great deal from nature".

Third of the four children, Alexander Fleming worked in a shipping office for four years. At the age of 21, he inherited some wealth from his uncle, John Fleming. One of his brothers, Tom, studied medicine and was opening a practice in London. Following his advice, he got enrolled in St. Mary's Hospital Medical School. In 1906, he successfully qualified with a MBBS degree.

In 1900, when the Boer War broke out, Fleming joined the Scottish regiment and served as a private where he excelled. His club captain advised him to opt for research rather than surgery. Later, he introduced Fleming to Sir Almroth Wright who agreed to take Fleming under his

guidance. So Fleming joined his research group where he served his entire life.

The idea for Penicillin first struck him during World War I, when Fleming worked as a Captain. He noticed that most of the soldiers died due to infections that resulted during the war rather than from battle-wounds. He observed that the antiseptics that were used to treats these wounds did more harm than good. After much research, he successfully discovered Penicillin.

Later he stated, "*When I woke up just after dawn on 28 September 1928, I certainly didn't plan to revolutionize all medicine by discovering the world's first antibiotic, or bacteria killer. But I suppose that was exactly what I did.*"

In recognition for his contribution, Alexander Fleming was knighted in 1944. In 1945, he was awarded the Nobel Prize in Physiology/Medicine.

Famous quotes:

• One sometimes finds what one is not looking for.

• It is the lone worker who makes the first advance in a subject; the details may be worked out by a team, but the prime idea is due to enterprise, thought, and perception of an individual.

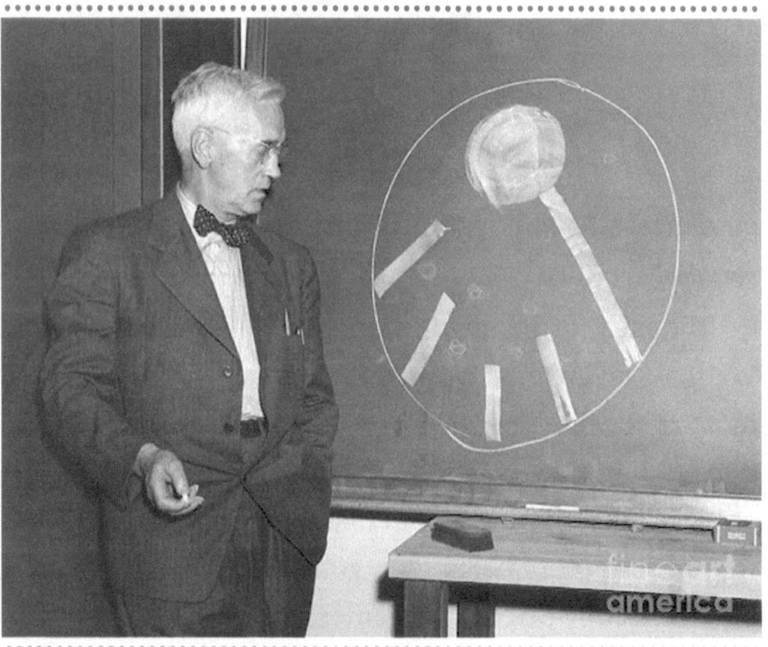

Chapter 14
Henry Ford

The founder of the Ford Motor Company, Henry Ford was born on 30 July 1863 in Dearborn, Michigan. From his early days, Ford was highly fascinated with machines. At the age of sixteen, he went to Detroit to find job in machine shops. During his work, he came across the internal combustion engine. Later he returned to the farm and worked as a part-time employee for the Westinghouse

Engine Company. Eventually in 1896, he constructed his first horseless carriage, which he sold in order to finance his work on building an improved model of the same.

In 1903, Ford incorporated the Ford Motor Company proclaiming, "I will build a car for the great multitude." He was able to accomplish this on October 1908, offering the Model T for $950. The Model T marked the beginning of the Motor Age.

Ford swirled a revolution in the manufacturing industry. In 1914, Ford began paying his employees five dollars a day, nearly doubling the wages offered by other manufacturers. He cut the workday from nine to eight hours, in order to convert the factory to a three-shift workday. Ford's mass-production techniques eventually led to the manufacture of a Model T every 24 seconds. His innovations acclaimed him as an international celebrity.

Ford's Model T irrevocably altered the American society. The urbanization patterns changed as more and more Americans owned cars. Ford witnessed many such changes during his lifetime, all the while longing for an agrarian lifestyle of his youth. In the years prior to his death on 7 April 1947, Ford sponsored the restoration of an idyllic rural town called Greenfield Village.

Famous quotes:

• If you think you can do a thing or think you can't do a thing, you're right.

• When everything seems to be going against you, remember that the airplane takes off against the wind, not with it.

Chapter 15
Galileo Galilei

Widely regarded as the 'Father of Modern Science', Galileo Galilei was born in Pisa, Italy on 15 February 1564. Upon his father's insistence, he pursued his medical degree but later shifted to his interests in mathematics and natural philosophy.

Shortly thereafter, at the age of 20, Galileo noticed a lamp swinging overhead while he was in a cathedral. Curious to find out how long it took the lamp to swing back and forth, he used his pulse to time large and small swings. Galileo discovered that the time interval between each swing was exactly the same. This discovery later came to be known as the law of the pendulum to be used to regulate clocks.

Faced with the need to somehow earn a living, Galileo started tutoring students in mathematics. He did some experimenting with floating objects, developing a balance that could tell him that a piece of gold was 19.3 times heavier than the same volume of water. He also earnestly

started campaigning for a position on the mathematics faculty at a major university.

In 1589, he obtained a chair of mathematics at the University of Pisa. Later, Galileo moved to the University of Padua. By 1593 he found himself in desperate need of additional cash. After his father died, the responsibility of his family fell on Galileo's shoulders. Debts were pressing down on him, most notably, the dowry for one of his sisters, which was paid in installments over decades.

What Galileo needed was to come up with some sort of device that could make him a tidy profit. He developed a rudimentary thermometer and an ingenious device to raise water from aquifers which found no market. He found greater success in 1596, with a military compass that could be used accurately to aim cannonballs. A modified civilian version that could be used for land surveying came out in 1597 and ended up earning a fair amount of money for Galileo.

It greatly helped him! Firstly, the instruments were sold for three times the cost of manufacture; secondly, he also offered classes on how to use the instrument and thirdly, the salary of the actual toolmaker was very less.

Galileo discovered the way to invent a telescope. He had other groundbreaking discoveries to his credit. He also discovered that the moon's surface was not smooth but uneven and rough.

Galileo was condemned to life imprisonment due to his obsession with the Copernicus theory. He later moved into a villa near Arcetri and spent the rest of his life there. He had an untimely death on 8 January 1634.

Famous quotes:

• You cannot teach a man anything; you can only help him find it within himself.

• All truths are easy to understand once they are discovered; the point is to discover them.

Chapter 16
Guglielmo Marconi

Acclaimed as the inventor of radio, Guglielmo Marconi was an Italian inventor and engineer, who proved the possibility of radio communication. He sent and received his first radio signal in Italy in 1895. By 1899, he flashed the first wireless signal across the English Channel and two years later received the letter 'S', telegraphed from England to Newfoundland. This was the first successful transatlantic radiotelegraph message in 1902.

In 1901, radiotelegraph service was instituted between five Hawaiian Islands. By 1903, a Marconi station located in Wellfleet, Massachusetts, carried an exchange or greetings between President Theodore Roosevelt and King Edward VII.

He received the Nobel Prize in 1909, making him one of the youngest Nobel laureates.

During World War I, governments began using radiotelegraph to be alert of the events, and to instruct the movements of troops and supplies. World War II

demonstrated the value of radio and encouraged its development. Radiotelegraph circuits to other countries enabled persons to communicate from practically any place on earth.

The first time the human voice was transmitted by radio is debatable. Claims range from the phrase, *"Hello Rainey"* spoken by Natan B. Stubblefield to a test partner near Murray in 1892, to an experimental program of talk and music by Reginald A. Fessenden of Massachusetts in 1906, which was heard by radio-equipped ships within several hundred miles.

In 1929, the high seas public radiotelephone service was inaugurated. At that time, telephone contact could be made only with ships within 1,500 miles of shore. Today, there is the ability to telephone nearly even- large ship, wherever it may be on the globe. In 1935, the first telephone call was made around the world, using a combination of wire and radio circuits.

Famous quotes:

• In the new era, thought itself will be transmitted by radio.

• The mystery of life is certainly the most persistent problem ever placed before the thought of man.

Chapter 17

James Clerk Maxwell

Regarded as one of the world's greatest physicists, James Clerk Maxwell was a Scottish physicist and mathematician. Maxwell's researches combined the fields of electricity and magnetism and introduced the concept of the electromagnetic field. Through his research, he showed the presence of magnetic field lines in a 'magnetic field'. If a bar magnet is placed on a magnetic field, it will experience magnetic forces, but the field exists even when no magnet is present. Similarly, an 'electric field' is the space in which electric forces may be sensed, for instance between metal objects charged (+) and (-) on a battery.

James Clerk Maxwell predicted the existence of radio waves. From this sprang the idea that light was an electric phenomenon, the discovery of radio waves, Einstein's theory of relativity and a great deal of present-day physics.

The largest telescope in the world is named after him 'The James Clerk Maxwell Telescope'. He died at the age of

48 due to abdominal cancer in 1879.

Famous quotes:

• Thoroughly conscious ignorance is the prelude to every real advance in science.

• It is of great advantage to the student of any subject to read the original memoirs on that subject, for science is always most completely assimilated when it is in the nascent state.

Chapter 18
Sir Isaac Newton

Isaac Newton was born in 1642, in a manor house in Lincolnshire, England. His father had died two months before his birth. When Isaac was three, his mother remarried and Isaac remained with his grandmother. He later pursued his studies in Cambridge University.

Isaac Newton explained the workings of the universe through mathematics. He formulated laws of motion and

gravitation through mathematical formulas to explain how objects move when a force acts on them.

Isaac published his most famous book, *Principia*, in 1687 while he was a mathematics professor at Trinity College, Cambridge. In the *Principia*, Isaac explained three basic laws that govern the way objects move. He then described his idea or theory, about gravity. Gravity is the force that causes things to fall down. If a pencil falls off a desk, it will land on the floor, not the ceiling. In his book, Isaac also used his laws to show that the planets revolve around the sun in orbits that are oval, not round.

Isaac Newton used three laws to explain the way objects move. They are called Newton's Laws. The First Law states that an object that is not pushed or pulled by any force will stay still or will keep moving in a straight line at a steady speed. It is easy to understand that a bike will not move unless something pushes or pulls it. If someone is riding a bike and jumps off before the bike is stopped, what happens? The bike continues on until it falls over. The tendency of an object to remain still or keep moving in a straight line, at a steady speed, is called inertia.

The Second Law explains how a force acts on an object. An object accelerates in the direction the force is moving it. If someone gets on a bike and pushes the pedals forward, the bike will begin to move. If someone gives the bike a push from behind, the bike will speed up.

The Third Law states that if an object is being pushed or pulled, it will push or pull equally in the opposite direction. If someone lifts a heavy box, they use force to push it up. The box is heavy because it is producing an equal force downwards on the lifter's arms.

Less than 50 years before Isaac Newton was born, it was thought that the planets were held in place by an invisible shield. Isaac proved that they were held in place by the sun's gravity. He also showed that the force of gravity was affected by 'distance and mass.' He was not the first to discover that the orbit of a planet was oval, but he was definitely the first one to explain how it worked.

Famous quotes:

• I can calculate the motion of heavenly bodies, but not the madness of people.

• To myself I am only a child playing on the beach, while vast oceans of truth lie undiscovered before me.

Chapter 19
Alfred Nobel

Alfred Nobel was born in Stockholm on 21 October 1833. His father, Immanuel Nobel, was an engineer and inventor who built bridges and buildings in Stockholm. In connection with his construction work, Immanuel Nobel also experimented with different techniques for blasting rocks.

When Nobel was eight, he along with his family moved to Russia. In Russia, his father opened a mechanical engineering workshop. From an early age, he was

interested in science, especially chemistry. In due course, he also acquired extensive literary and philosophical knowledge and mastered several foreign languages. He mostly studied on his own, and was never enrolled in any form of formal education system.

He returned to Sweden in 1863 and began working as a chemist at his father's workshop at Heleneborg in Stockholm. He succeeded in further developing the explosive nitroglycerine, which he began manufacturing in Sweden in 1864. In 1867, Nobel obtained a patent on a special type of nitroglycerine, which he called 'dynamite'. The invention of 'dynamite' proved its usefulness in the field of construction and building in many countries. The original form of dynamite was gradually replaced by gelatin dynamite, which was comparatively safer to handle.

He went on experimenting, in pursuit of inventions in many fields, notably with synthetic materials. He became one of the wealthiest men in Europe as he highly earned from many enterprises all over the world.

He lived in Paris for a number of years, but had planned to return to Sweden and settle down for good at Karlskoga, where he owned some property. But before he could act upon his plans, he died at his home in San Remo in Italy on 10 December 1896.

In January 1897, it was learned that he had left a bulk of his considerable estate to a fund, the interest on which was to be awarded annually to the persons whose work had been of the greatest benefit to mankind. The statutes of the foundation which administered the fund, the Nobel Foundation, were adopted on 29 June 1900.

At last he was successful in serving the mankind as he willed his fortune for the betterment of the society by acknowledging significant contributions in the fields of Physics, Chemistry, Physiology or Medicine, Literature and Peace.

Famous quotes:

• If I have a thousand ideas and only one turns out to be good, I am satisfied.

• Hope is nature's veil for hiding truth's nakedness.

Chapter 20
Louis Pasteur

Widely known as one of the 'Fathers of Germ Theory', Louis Pasteur was born on 21 December 1822 in Dole France. He was married to Marie Laurent and the couple had five children. Three of his children died of typhoid fever which led Pasteur to find a cure for the disease. He graduated in 1842 from Besancon College Royal de la tranche and later attended Ecole Normale to study Physics and Chemistry, specializing in crystals. In his early research, Pasteur worked with the wine growers of France, helping with the fermentation process to develop a way to pasteurize and kill germs.

Pasteur then worked within the textile industry, finding a cure for a disease affecting silk worms. Pasteur also discovered cures for chicken cholera, anthrax and rabies. The Pasteur Institute was opened in 1888. During Pasteur's lifetime, it was extremely difficult for him to convince others to believe in his ideas. Pasteur fought to convince surgeons that germs existed and these germs carried diseases. He raised awareness against the use of

dirty instruments and unclean hands which spread germs and thus spreads diseases. Pasteur's pasteurization process kills germs and prevents the spread of diseases.

Pasteur's primary contributions to microbiology and medicine were in instituting changes in hospital and medical practices to minimize the disease outbreak by microbes or germs. He discovered that weak forms of disease could be used as an immunization to fight against stronger forms of that particular disease. He also discovered that rabies was transmitted by viruses too small to be seen under the microscopes of the time. Thus, he introduced the concept of viruses to the medical world.

He also suggested that spoilage of perishable products could be prevented by destroying the microbes already present. Pasteur applied this theory to the preservation of beverages and foodstuffs, introducing the technique of heat treatment, now known as pasteurization.

Famous quotes:

• In the fields of observation chance favors only the prepared mind.

• Let me tell you the secret that has led me to my goal. My strength lies solely in my tenacity.

Chapter 21
Blaise Pascal

Blaise Pascal, the French scientist was one of the most reputed mathematician and physicist of his time. He is credited with inventing an early calculator, amazingly advanced for its time. Blaise Pascal composed a treatise on the communication of sounds at the age of twelve and composed a treatise on conic sections at the age of sixteen.

Blaise Pascal was born at Clermont on 19 June 1623 and died at Paris on 19 August 1662. His father was a local judge and tax collector at Clermont who moved to Paris in 1631, partly to prosecute his own scientific studies

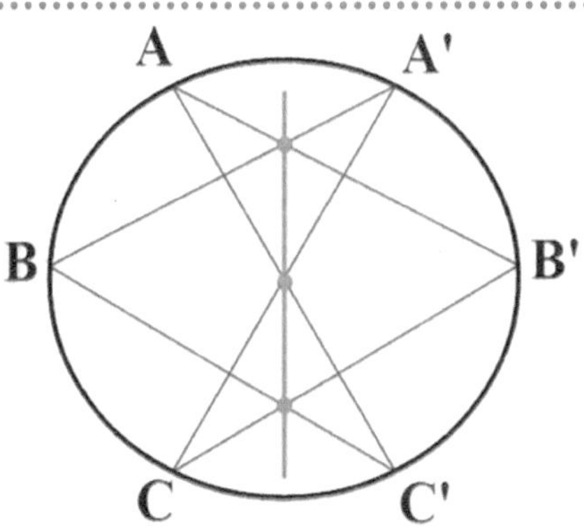

and partly to carry on the education of his only son, who displayed exceptional ability. Blaise Pascal was kept at home, in order to ensure that he is not being overworked. It was directed that his education should be confined to the study of languages and should not include any mathematics.

This naturally excited the boy's curiosity and one day, he asked, "What is geometry?" His tutor replied that it was the science of constructing exact figures and of determining the proportions between different parts of a figure. Blaise Pascal got curious and gave up his play-time to study geometry. In a few weeks, he discovered many properties of figures and in particular, the proposition that the sum of the angles of a triangle is equal to two right angles.

At the age of fourteen, Blaise Pascal was admitted to the weekly meetings of Roberval, Merscnne, Mydorge and other French geometricians, who formed the French Academy. At sixteen, he wrote an essay on conic sections and in 1641, at the age of eighteen; he constructed the first arithmetical machine, an instrument which he further improved eight years later. His correspondence with Fermat showed his interest in analytical geometry and physics.

He was meditating marriage when an accident turned his thoughts towards a religious life. Believing in mysticism, he considered incidents like this as special summons to abandon the world. He wrote an account of the accident on a small piece of parchment and wore next to his heart, to perpetually remind him of his covenant. He moved to Port Royal, where he continued to live until his death in 1662. His incessant study affected his health. He suffered from insomnia and acute dyspepsia which started at the age of seventeen or eighteen and was physically worn out at the time of his death.

Famous quotes:

- We know the truth, not only by the reason, but also by the heart.

- Kind words do not cost much. Yet they accomplish much.

- The knowledge of God is very far from the love of Him.

$$\cdots\cdots\cdots\cdots\cdots\cdots\cdots\cdots\cdots\cdots\cdots\cdots\cdots$$

Chapter 22

Percy L. Spencer

Spencer, born in Howland, Maine, was orphaned at a young age. Although he never graduated from grammar school, he became the Senior Vice President and a member of the Board of Directors at Raytheon, receiving ISO patents during his career. Because of his accomplishments, Spencer was awarded the Distinguished Service Medal by the U.S. Navy and has a building named after him at Raytheon.

Shortly after the end of World War II, Percy Spencer, famously known as an electronics genius and war hero, was touring one of his laboratories at the Raytheon Company. He stopped momentarily in front of a magnetron, the power tube that drives a radar set. Feeling a sudden and strange sensation, Spencer noticed that the chocolate bar in his pocket had begun to melt.

So, he did what any good inventor would — he thought of experimenting with some unpopped popcorn. Holding the bag of corn next to the magnetron, Spencer watched as the kernels exploded into puffy white morsels.

From this simple experiment, Spencer and Raytheon developed the microwave oven! The first microwave oven weighed a hefty 750 pounds and stood five feet, six inches. At first, it was used exclusively in restaurants, railroad cars and ocean liners — places where large quantities of food had to be cooked.

But, the oven had several shortcomings. The meat refused to brown, even the french fries looked white and limp. To make matters worse, Raytheon chairman,

Charles Adams' cook quit because Adams demanded him to prepare food using a microwave oven.

In fact, it took decades to refine the microwave oven to a point where it would be useful to an average consumer. Today, Percy Spencer's radar boxes melt chocolate and pops popcorn in millions of homes around the world.

In 1945, Spencer created a device to cook food using microwave radiation. Raytheon saw the possibilities and after acquiring Amana Refrigeration in 1965, it was able to sell microwave ovens on a large scale. The first microwave oven was called the Radarange. Today, there are over 200 million in use throughout the world!

Famous quote:

• I just got hold of a lot of textbooks and taught myself while I was standing at night.

Chapter 23

Wright Brothers

In 1899, after Wilbur Wright had written a letter of request to the Smithsonian Institution for information about flight experiments, the Wright Brothers designed their first aircraft. It was small, biplane glider, flown as a kite to test their solution for controlling the craft by Wing warping. Wing Warping is a method of arching the wingtips slightly, to control the aircraft's rolling motion and balance.

The Wrights spent a great deal of their time observing birds in flight. They noticed that the birds soared into the wind and that the air flowing over the curved surface of their wings lifts them in the air. Birds change the shape of their wings to turn and maneuver. They believed that they could use this technique to obtain roll control by warping or changing the shape of a portion of the wing.

Following a successful glider test, the Wrights built and tested a full-size glider. They selected Kitty Hawk, North Carolina as their test site because it was remotely located.

In 1900, the Wrights successfully tested their new 50-pound biplane glider with its 17-foot wingspan and wing-warping mechanism at Kitty Hawk, in both unmanned and piloted flights. In fact, it was the first piloted glider. Based upon the results, the Wright Brothers planned to refine the controls and landing gear and build a bigger glider.

In 1901, at Kill Devil Hills, North Carolina, the Wright Brothers flew the largest glider ever flown, with a 22-foot wingspan, a weight of nearly 100 pounds and which skids for landing. However, this model encountered many problems. The wings did not have enough lifting power, the forward elevator was not effective in controlling the pitch and the wing-warping mechanism occasionally caused the airplane to spin out of control. Disappointed, they thought that probably man would never be able to fly in their lifetime.

In spite of such problems, the Wrights reviewed their test results and determined that the calculations they had used were not reliable. They planned to design a new glider with a 32-feet wingspan and a tail to help stabilize it.

During 1902, the brothers flew numerous test glides using their new glider. Their studies showed that a movable tail would help balance the craft and its weight. Therefore, the Brothers connected a movable tail to the wing-warping wires, to coordinate turns. With successful glides to verify their wind tunnel tests, the inventors planned to build a powered aircraft.

The brothers built a movable track to help launch the Flyer. This downhill track would help the aircraft to gain enough airspeed to fly. After two attempts to fly this machine, Orville Wright successfully took the Flyer for a 12-second, sustained flight on 17 December 1903. This was the first successful, powered, piloted flight in history.

Famous quotes:

• The airplane stays up because it does not have the time to fall.

• If birds can glide for long periods of time, then… why can't I?

Chapter 24

James Watt

James Watt is an eminent British engineer and mechanical inventor. He was born at Greenock, in 1736. Watt developed extraordinary talents in practical mechanics and perfected his grand discovery of condensing the steam by means of an airtight cylinder.

In 1765, James Watt, while working for the University of Glasgow, was assigned the task of repairing a Newcomen engine, which was deemed inefficient. Watt started working to improve the Newcomen's design. Most notable was Watt's 1769 patent for a separate condenser connected to a cylinder by a valve. Unlike Newcomen's engine, the condenser could be cooled down while the cylinder was hot. Watt's engine became the dominant design for all steam engines.

He was famous for his improvements in the steam engine and for coining the term 'horsepower'. The SI unit of power, the Watt, is named after him.

In 1773, Watt entered into a partnership with Matthew Boulton of Soho, near Birmingham, when the manufacture of the new engines was commenced at Soho Iron Works.

For some years, Watt occupied himself in the surveying and engineering public works in Scotland. He retired from business in the year 1800, handing his extensive business which Boulton had created at Soho, in the interests of both his sons. He died at Heathfield, in Staffordshire on 25 August 1819.

Famous quotes:

• I can think of nothing else than this machine.

• A lie can run around the world before the truth can get its boots on.